Cars, Cars, C...

Michael Steer

Contents

Changing the World	2	Problems with Cars	14
First Cars	4	No Petrol!	16
Cars and More Cars	8	Fast Cars	20
Cars Everywhere!	10	Cars are Stars!	22
All Kinds of Cars	12	Glossary	24

Changing the World

Cars have changed how we live.

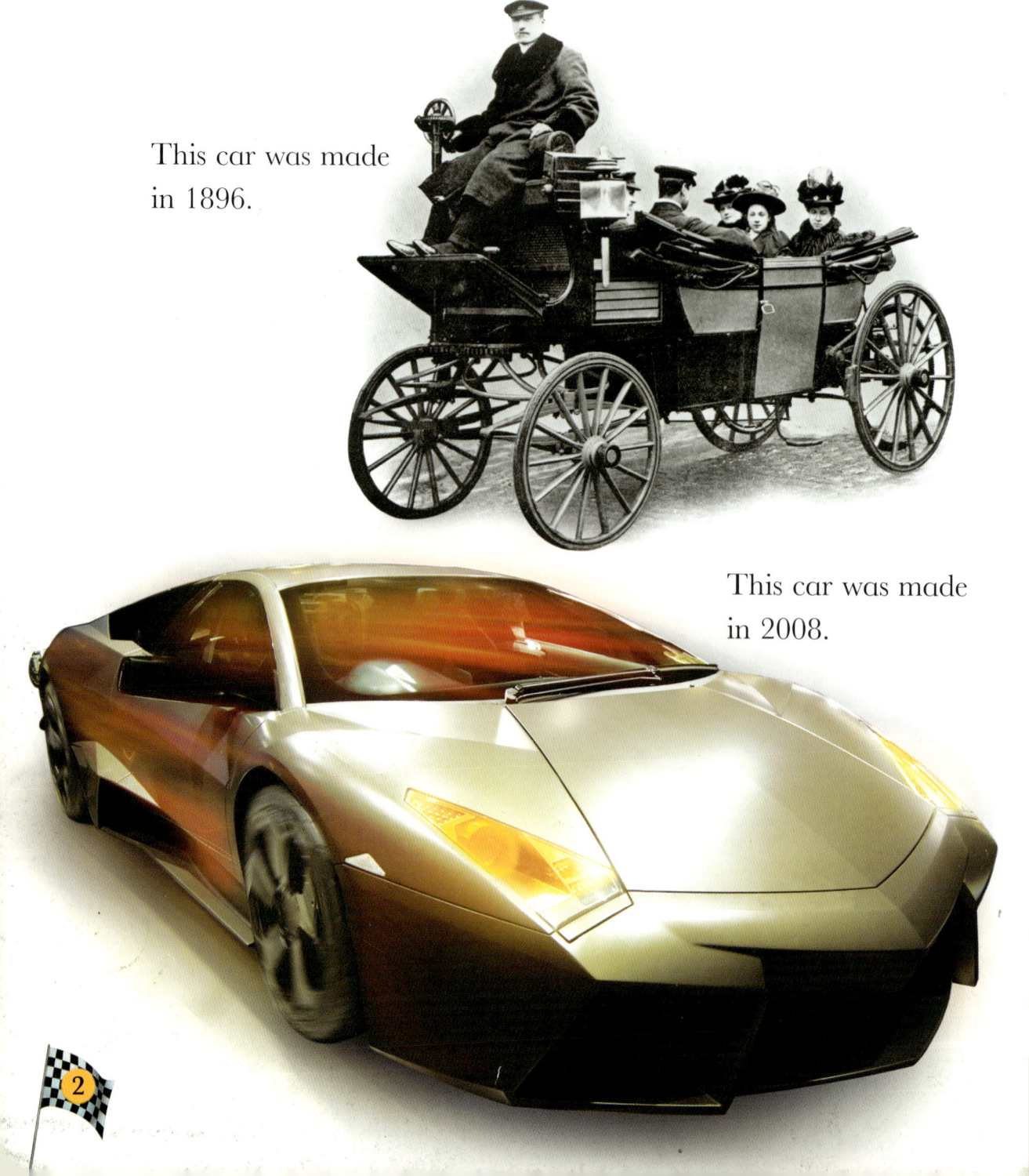

This car was made in 1896.

This car was made in 2008.

Cars have also changed how we get to places.

Long ago, people used carts to get from place to place.

First Cars

The first car used **steam** to make it go.
It was very slow. It was built over 200 years ago.

The First Car Crash
The first steam car crashed into a wall.

The first car that used **petrol** was made around 120 years ago.

Most people could walk faster than the first petrol car!

In the early 1900s, not many people had a car. Cars cost a lot of money.

An American called Henry Ford wanted everyone to be able to buy a car. Cars were made quickly and **cheaply** at his **factory**.

Henry Ford driving the first car he built in 1896

The Model T Ford was made in Henry Ford's factory around 100 years ago.

Cars and More Cars

By 1912, hundreds of cars were being made each day. Today, thousands and thousands of cars are made each day.

Today, robots help to make cars.

robot arms

paint

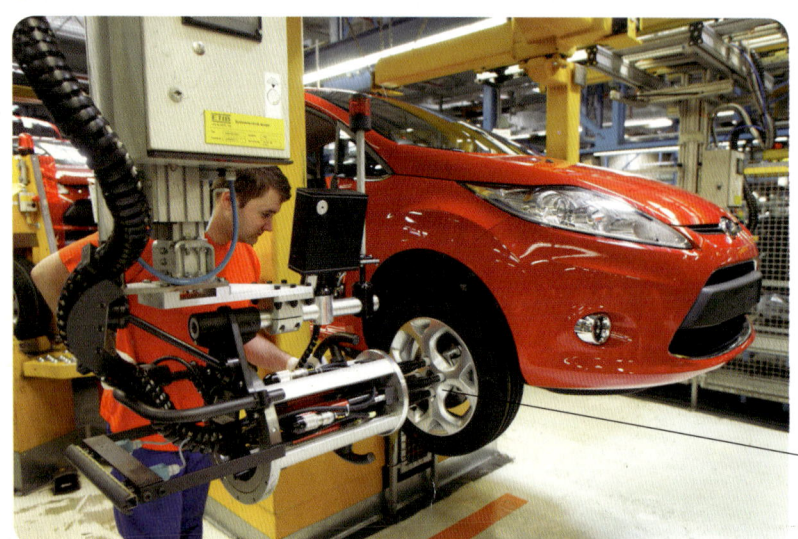

Putting wheel nuts on the car

Shaping Up

The first cars looked nice but they could not go fast. Today, cars can look good and go fast, too!

a 1926 Morris Oxford

a Lamborghini Murcielago

Cars Everywhere!

Cars changed how people lived. People drove to places instead of walking to them. They even drove their cars on holidays.

People even went to see films and stayed in their cars!

Just Drive In!
Today you can wash your car and buy food without getting out of your car.

All Kinds of Cars

Today, there are many kinds of cars. There are:

4-wheel-drive cars

mini cars

funny-looking cars

racing cars

family cars

A Car or a Boat?

This car can drive on the road and float on the water. It can even go under the water like a submarine!

Problems with Cars

There are over 600 million cars in the world. All these cars use a lot of petrol. Using a lot of petrol is bad for the Earth.

Big Problem 1

Cars need petrol to go. Petrol burns inside the engines and makes smoke. This smoke has bad gases which cause **air pollution.** It can make people and animals sick.

Big Problem 2

Petrol is made from oil. Oil is made under the ground – it takes millions of years. Once oil runs out, petrol will run out. How will we make cars go if there is no petrol?

To fix these problems, cars need to change.

No Petrol!

Today, some new cars use less petrol or no petrol at all!

These cars use electricity and petrol to make them go.

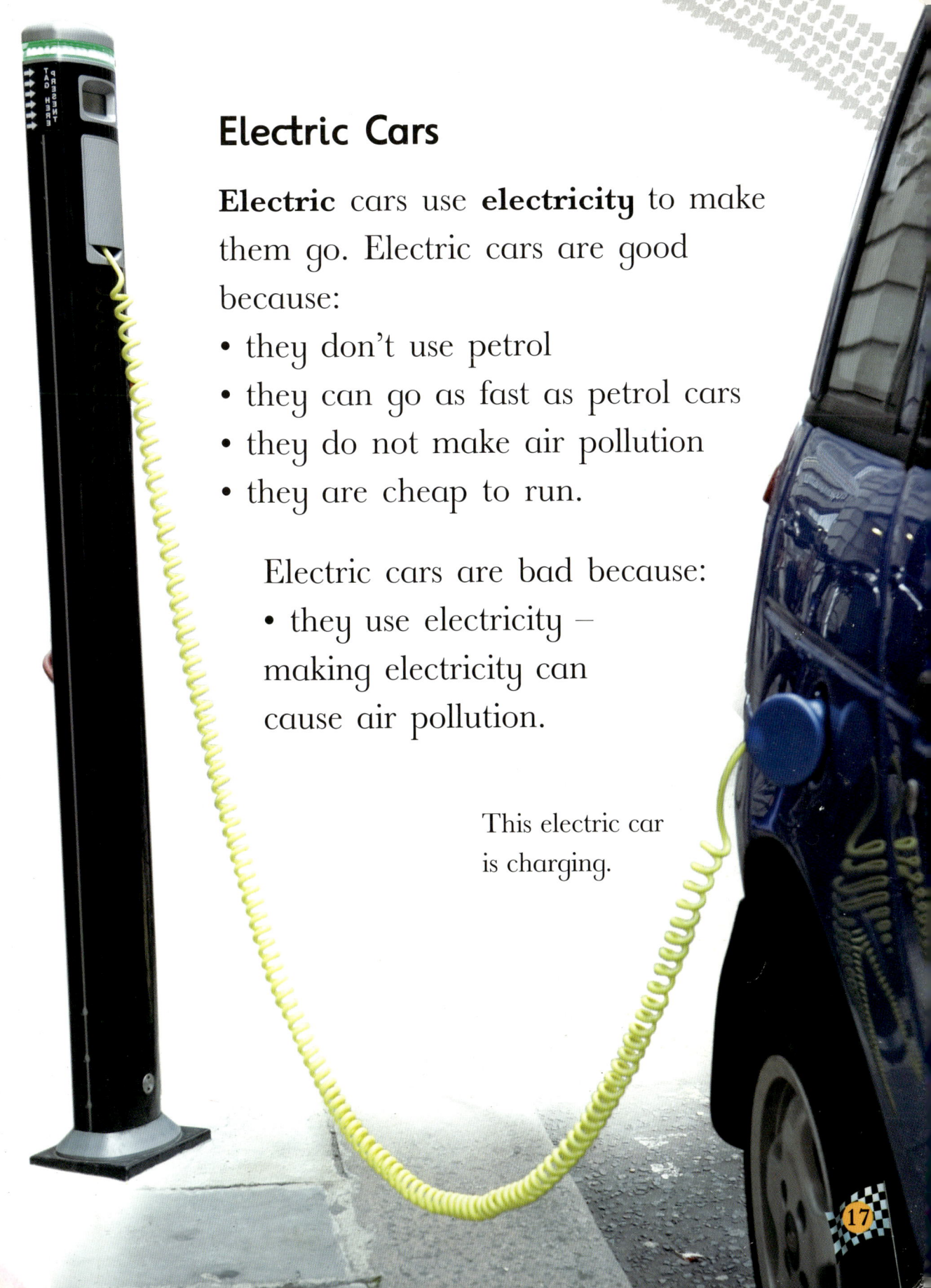

Electric Cars

Electric cars use **electricity** to make them go. Electric cars are good because:
- they don't use petrol
- they can go as fast as petrol cars
- they do not make air pollution
- they are cheap to run.

Electric cars are bad because:
- they use electricity – making electricity can cause air pollution.

This electric car is charging.

Solar Cars

Solar cars use **energy** from the sun to make them go. Solar cars are good because:
- they do not use petrol
- they do not make air pollution
- they are cheap to run.

a solar racing car

Solar cars are bad because:
- they go very slowly
- they use **batteries** – making batteries can cause air pollution.

The First Solar Car
The first solar car was made in 1955. It was called the Sun-mobile!

Fast Cars

Some cars are made to go very, very fast. They can travel almost as fast as a jet plane. **Wow!**

Formula One racing car

How Fast?

a racing car — over 360 km an hour

a car today — 225 km an hour

the Model T-Ford — 72 km an hour

a person walking — 6.5 km an hour

That's Fast!
This car can travel at around 400 kilometres an hour!

Cars Are Stars!

Cars come in many shapes, sizes and colours.

Who knows what cars will be like in the future? Maybe you will get in your car and fly away!

Glossary

air pollution
bad gases in smoke that go into the air, which are bad for you and the planet

batteries
items that hold electricity

cheaply
not costing a lot

electric
getting energy from electricity

electricity
electric power, or current

energy
power like solar power or electricity

factory
place where something is made

petrol
fuel used in some engines to make them go

solar
getting energy from the sun

steam
mist in the air made from boiling water

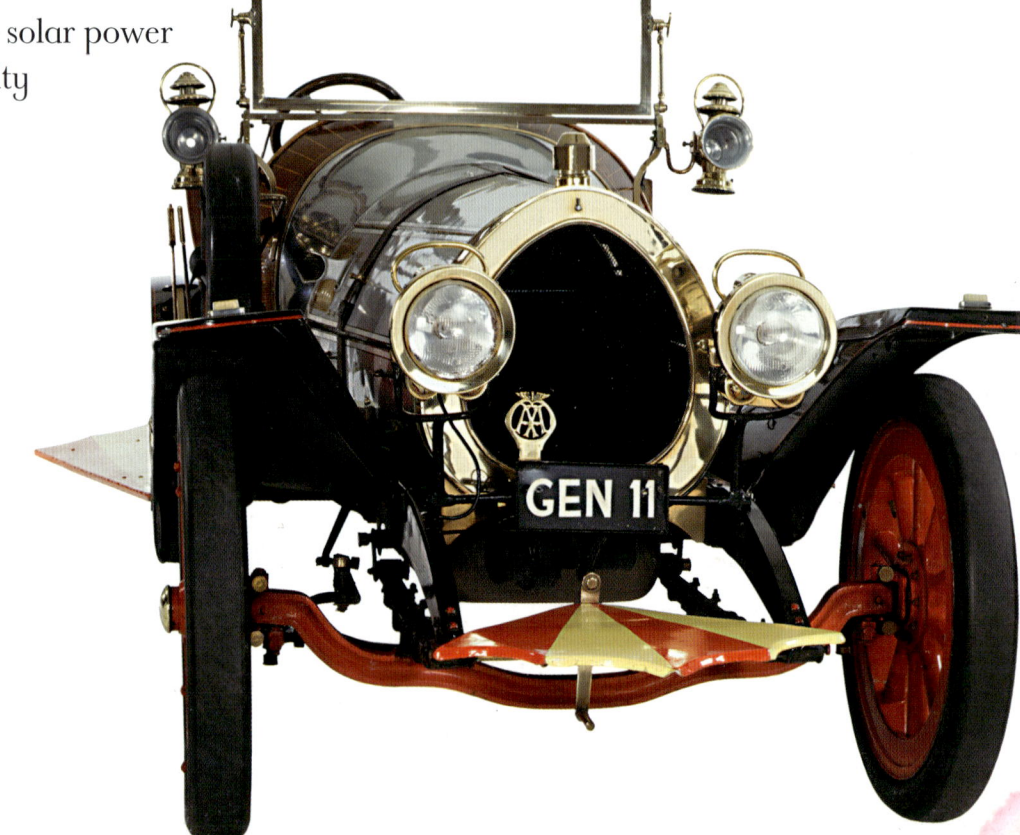